EMERGE INTO
GROWTH

THE FULFILLMENT CYCLE

EMERGE INTO
GROWTH

Book 1: Learning

RICHARD-ANTHONY PANIER

CONTENTS

DEDICATION

This book is dedicated to my unborn grandchildren. I hope it inspires you to strive toward becoming your best self and living a meaningful life.

Our lineage tells a story of building, growing, and creating opportunities: my great-grandfather built homes; my grandfather was a landlord of farmland in Haiti; my father was a real estate & mortgage broker who also owned property; and I am building properties, providing shelter to those in need, brokering deals, and teaching others how to generate wealth through real estate.

Whatever your passion may be, let real estate be the foundation that funds your dreams.

INTRODUCTION

What if I told you that becoming the best version of yourself isn't complicated or as strenuous as it seems? Imagine life as a game. Like the main character in Grand Theft Auto, but instead of wreaking havoc, you unlock simplified cheat codes of personal development that propel you towards your goals faster, more efficiently, and with a sense of control of your life's destiny. All you have to do is learn, apply, and repeat the cheat codes.

Before we dive into unlocking the cheat codes of personal development, there are foundational concepts you need to understand– principles that will prepare you for the journey ahead. We essentially need to get comfortable with the controller's buttons before trying to input the codes.

Human energy is finite without some rest and intentional preservation. Think of your mental, physical, and emotional resources like a rechargeable battery: they deplete with overuse and must be consciously conserved when possible. Willpower withers under strain, discipline erodes over time, and too many choices can spiral into chaos, all stemming from decision fatigue. The key is to conserve your energy and direct it to what matters most.

There are names you have heard before: Serena Williams, Barack Obama, and Steve Jobs who have famously reduced decision fatigue by limiting the number of choices in their daily routines. This allows them to focus their energy on more important tasks. Serena had consistent routines before matches to eliminate decision making and to stay sharp before walking on to the court. Barack admitted in an interview to wearing navy or grey suits during presidency to pare down decisions stating he has too many other decisions to make. We all know the infamous Steve Jobs uniform: black turtleneck, blue jeans, and dad sneakers. Each of these great individuals were on the same page of minimizing unnecessary decisions.

The Fulfillment Cycle's three pillars allow you to have an easy philosophy to maneuver through life. Similar to the branches of government, the legs of a stool, or the components of an atom (electron, proton, neutron) life's cheat codes can be made into digestible parts of three. In Book 1, the theme is Liquidity, learning as the foundation for growth and transformation. Learning is broken down into a framework on mastering the mind (Mindset), understanding the self (Identity), and exploring potential (Exploration).

SECTION 1

Mindset

CHAPTER 1

Thoughts

"As one thinketh in their heart, so are they."
—Proverbs 23:7

Thoughts, the foundation of everything. They precede actions, those actions shape our habits, and habits (subconscious responses) define our character. However, not all thoughts are created equal. How we think about ourselves and the world around us profoundly impacts our effort, our success, our happiness, and our resilience. In this chapter, I will explore how self-talk, perception, and beliefs about myself shape the trajectory of our lives; and how gaining control over our thoughts is one of the most powerful shifts we can make.

The shift that changed everything. My first major mindset shift happened when I moved during my freshman year of high school to West Palm Beach to live with my dad. Around that time, he started reading self-help books like *The 7 Habits of Highly Successful People* and *Think and Grow Rich* that really stuck with him. He began to pass along those lessons to me. But the more profound influence wasn't what he said. It was how he *saw* me.

My mother gave me a pretty strong foundation of manners, spontaneity, and grit but never let me see us struggle. She was an empath and typically the life of the party or the hostess with the mostess. My father on the other hand came to the U.S. at 16, alone. He had a couple hundred dollars to his name as emergency money to buy a flight back to Haiti if he couldn't make it work stateside. So when I moved in with my father around that same age but different lifestyle he didn't get it. I was spending money on sneakers, playing basketball for leisure, and going to parties. Even while holding two jobs and doing alright in school, he thought I was wasting my life. That stuck with me, he didn't peep my duality.

He didn't believe I was taking life seriously. And although it hurt, it also sparked something in me.

I made a decision: I'll prove him wrong, but not at the cost of my joy or childhood.

Before graduating high school, I sold my PS2 and most of my sneaker collection to mentally prepare for the next chapter, college. I didn't have the words for it back then, but I knew I was stepping into something different. At the time I figured I was "putting away childish things" but in reality I was just clearing my environment of distractions. Freshman year at FAMU was a bit of a roller coaster due to my social nature and newfound freedom. My grades slipped a bit and I lost a $350 semester scholarship and I knew better than to lose money! So another shift came sophomore year of college when I picked up *As a Man Thinketh* by James Allen. It was short, but it hit me deeply. That snowflake began to snowball and I realized I was thinking too small. Simply changing my external surroundings wasn't going to be enough, I needed to change my internal perspective.

I began to speak differently. Not just to others, but to myself. I refrained from cursing around women and children, which was challenging because I had to be able to turn it on and off in different settings. My vocabulary expanded from that decision and from reading because it forced me to find alternative and creative ways to express myself. I began looking for the positive in most situations. Others began to gravitate towards me because I spoke life into them and myself. I believed more in what I could become, not just what I currently was. That one mindset shift laid the foundation for everything that came next.

Self-talk and the inner script. The most important conversations you have each day are not with others, they are with yourself. That ongoing dialogue becomes the script that shapes your daily experience. Positive self-talk empowers, uplifts, and moves you forward. Negative self-talk sabotages confidence, paralyzes effort, and stops you from even trying.

"I could never do that."

"Why even bother?"

"I'm not good enough."

"That's just the way I am."

"Whether you think you can or think you can't, you're right."
–Henry Ford.

These thoughts, left unchecked, grow roots. They become truths we never meant to believe. I understand thoughts will come and go, including negative ones. The key isn't to suppress them, it's to catch them before they take root, before they become a part of your beliefs. So I began to say yes to every opportunity that could have a positive outcome even if it scared me.

One powerful reminder I carry with me is: **"Don't believe everything you think."**

Planting the right seeds. After reading *Rich Dad, Poor Dad*, I stopped saying "I can't" and started asking, "How can I?" That one shift reprogrammed my brain. It forced me into possibility, into creativity, and into movement. I got involved with the National Association of Black Accountants as the President's assistant and later became the president myself and served two terms increasing membership 3 fold.

I developed my personal mantra:

Happy. Healthy. Wealthy.

- **Happy** became a mood I chose each morning and built into habit.

- **Healthy** became a commitment to a processing emotions, exercising routinely, eating to fuel, and sleeping to recover

- **Wealthy** became the pursuit of abundant resources: relationships, knowledge, and money.

Fake it til you make it! This saying has scientific backing on studies between the connection of emotions and physical actions like adopting a smile even when you aren't feeling happy. I began smiling in the mirror for no reason and that usually caused me to laugh at myself and feel real joy. Try it. Similar to power poses, confident and expansive postures like putting your hands behind your head with your elbows facing outward is found to make people feel powerful in their environment and reduce stress. Yet, still be considerate, don't manspread on the subway.

I started treating my mind like a garden. Positive thoughts were seeds. Negative thoughts? Weeds. I didn't pretend the negative didn't exist, I just didn't let them grow unchecked.

I found value in stoic principles too from books like *Meditations* by Marcus Aurelius. Not to become emotionless, but learning to pause, to respond instead of react. I was a hothead as a child, constantly getting into fights. It was imperative that I learned to regulate my emotions before I came across the wrong scenario and ended up dead or in jail.

I meditated. I journaled. I affirmed what I wanted to believe, until it became real. These three quotes from the book stuck with me the most:

"You have power over your mind, not external factors. Realize this and you will find strength."

"The happiness in your life depends on the quality of your thoughts." #Bars

"Everything we hear is an opinion, not a fact. Everything we see is a perspective, not the truth."

Dreaming is better than nothing. Studies show that people are happier before they win the lottery than after. Why? Because the act of buying a lottery ticket allows them to dream.

Even though the odds are slim, the possibility lights them up. But after winning, you're weighed down by the responsibility that comes with the money, which you probably left that reality out of the dream.

That same principle applies to life. Dreaming and taking small actions often brings more joy than doing nothing at all.

You don't need a guaranteed outcome to move forward.

You just need to *conceive* a thought, a mindset that *believes*, and take action to *achieve*. My goal in college was to get a great paying job offer in NYC, and I did just that via two full-time offers before I walked at graduation.

Realism vs. Pessimism. Another common trap in our thinking is confusing **realism** with **pessimism**.

Pessimism sees the problem and stops there. They are problem-spotters. Realism acknowledges the challenge *and* looks for a way through or around it. They are problem-solvers.

Problem-spotters add no real value, just point out the elephant in the room. Problem-solvers are high value individuals 'cause they can keep the ball moving!

For example:

"I can't afford that" closes the door.

"How can I afford that?" has you looking for the key.

A problem-focused mind gets stuck. A solution-focused mind makes strides. That single shift, from blocker to builder, can change your entire direction. My father has been in real estate since my middle school years. I knew once I lived out my college days I'd do the same.

For many businesses like real estate there are 3 resources you need to get started: money, knowledge, and time. I had time but no tangible experience and not enough money. The cool thing is, if you have two, you can borrow the third. Since I only had one, it was time for me to grind.

I originally had an offer with a big four accounting firm. I was their campus ambassador, reigning in students left and right for internships and full-time roles but I wanted more so I pivoted to a big bank that offered a higher salary and a $10k sign-on bonus, bingo! My seed money to invest in real estate.

Growth mindset: Reclaiming the Beginner's Fire. Dr. Carol Dweck's research in her book, *Mindset*, taught me that how we *view* our abilities defines our path.

A fixed mindset says, "That's just how I am."

A growth mindset says, "I can learn to get better."

As babies, we all had growth mindsets.

Imagine a baby saying to themselves, "I've never walked before, so I won't try." It sounds absurd, right? They even fall dozens, if not hundreds, of times. But they don't give up. They may pause but they eventually try again.

Somewhere along the way, adults lose that spirit. We fear the fall. We protect our pride. But the truth is: just because you've never done something doesn't mean you can't master it. A fine example would be speaking another language or real estate investing. Just because something is difficult at first, doesn't mean it can't be simplified to get to the end.

You are not your mistakes. After college, I didn't have any student loans. I made it a point every Saturday morning to apply for scholarships even while I matriculated through FAMU. However, I paid off what I thought was a mountain of credit card debt, a whopping $400, after being hit with interest on it.

Down the line I loaned $4,000 to a friend to grow his barbershop, and when it failed, he stopped paying.

Later, I lost over $40,000 to a lawsuit stemming from one of my rental properties. I was carrying coverage for the property but not proper coverage for liability to cover my property managers who were the true defendants in the case. The details were absurd, the claim was fake, but the cost was real. From $400 to $4,000 to $40,000; as I grew it seemed that each new problem would too. When Biggie said, "More money, more problems," he wasn't lying!

Mental fortitude is a must. If you fold under pressure you'll never learn the lesson or get mentally tougher. I learned not to isolate each situation as bad or good but an occurrence that I would learn from. Loss vs Lesson. It's only a loss if you don't learn from it. I could have paid $40k in tuition to learn or in the real world, and I chose the real world because it came with real assets if I made the right moves.

Nonetheless, that season rocked me. But my father said something that changed my outlook:

"If you had nothing, you can't lose anything. You've reached a level that people envy. A level that requires responsibility and with that comes pressure to maintain pleasure."

That reminded me: **I am not defined by my losses. I am defined by how I respond to them.**

Persistence with flexibility. Thoughts don't just start the journey, they sustain it.

Persistence is the fuel that keeps me going when things get hard. But persistence without flexibility is burnout. Life will throw detours. You'll have to pivot. That doesn't mean you've failed, it means you're human. Consider a GPS. You put in the destination, and if a road is closed, it reroutes you. It doesn't cancel the trip.

Stay focused on the destination, but stay open to an alternative path. The easiest way is to ask who has been, such as mentors, teachers, or authors. Ask yourself questions that open doors rather than closes them. Hindsight is 20/20 so ask those who went before you.

Thoughts become things. Your mindset is your map. Your actions are your vehicle. Your persistence is the fuel. So the real question becomes: *Where will you choose to go?* Because every journey starts with a single thought.

Make sure yours is one worth following.

C H A P T E R   2

Awareness

*We can be blind to the obvious, and we are
also blind to our own blindness.*
—Daniel Kahneman

The power of presence. Awareness is less complicated than you think, but deeper than you know. It's not just about being mindful. It's about recognizing where your attention is going and where it's needed most. It's noticing what's influencing your thoughts, emotions, and actions. And it's learning to pause long enough to ask: *What am I feeling? Why am I feeling it? And what does this moment require of me?*

Awareness is the key that unlocks growth because without it, you can't acknowledge that growth is needed. Many grasp the concept but struggle with the practice.

We live in a world full of distractions, endless information, and quick reactions. It's easy to move on autopilot. Doing what we've always done. Reacting based on emotion, habit, or carelessness. Awareness challenges that rhythm. It interrupts it. Awareness, in its fullest form, spans three dimensions:

- **Self:** knowing what's happening inside of you when it comes to thoughts, feelings, and physically

- **Spatial:** understanding your environment and how you show up in that space

- **Temporal:** using the limited time you have with clarity and intentionality

Mastering awareness doesn't happen overnight. But every time you notice something you used to overlook, you take a step closer to it.

Self-Awareness: The Inner Mirror. My earliest encounters with self-awareness came as a child. Whenever I got in trouble, my mother wouldn't just discipline me, she'd send me to my room with a simple assignment, "Go think about what you did." I was forced to ask myself "Why'd I do it?" or "What was my thought process?" Reflecting on how to spot the pattern and not to make the same mistake again. That habit of internal review stuck with me. I'm now to the point where I can ask myself that question before I act and speak. I uplift more and offend less while still getting my point across.

Even deeper, at five years old, I had to process something much bigger: my parents' divorce. At first, I could only feel my own pain. But then something shifted as years passed and reflection came into play, I could see my mother's pain. Then I began to wonder how not just my mother but also my father was feeling or "why'd he do it?" That shift, from being *in it* to *observing it*, is what self-awareness does. It stretches you beyond your own ego and into others' perspectives. Quick judgements often lead to unregulated emotions and a *reaction*. Understand that your emotions are temporary but your actions and words can have everlasting effects. Each moment you pause, better prepares you for the next one, allowing you to *respond*.

I found similar clarity in poetry, writing lyrics, and later through journaling. Writing became a safe space to witness my thoughts without judgement, track emotional patterns, and release mental clutter. Eventually, I discovered breathwork and meditation, which brought even more stillness.

Self-Awareness doesn't make you perfect, it makes you confront your own feelings.

Spatial Awareness: Reading the room, holding your energy. Spatial awareness is the skill of understanding how your presence affects the space around you, and how others' energy affects you. One of my favorite practices is not using my phone the first few hours of the day. (If that seems too difficult or you can't see the point, you may want to read *Digital Minimalism.*) It allows my own thoughts, not text messages, not emails, not timelines to guide my mental tone. Who are you without outside influence? Silence creates space for awareness to rise.

I also study body language and nonverbal cues. I once took notes from a podcast on Charisma that explained the subtle dance between warmth and competence:

- During conversation lean in slightly, angle your body toward the person talking, use downward vocal inflection—these convey confidence.

- Tilt your head, nod, react with gentle "mmhmms" or soft laughs because these create comfort and connection.

These are things you can only notice when you're truly present. That's why charisma isn't just about speaking, it's about seeing. Spatial awareness helps you move intentionally, not just physically, but energetically. Are you a joy or comfortable to be around?

Temporal Awareness: Time is a canvas. Time isn't just something you manage. It's something sacred. As we grow older, it feels like time speeds up. That's because routine compresses our sense of time. When we don't have to pay attention the world whizzes by. But you can slow time down by creating new experiences, deeper presence, or moments of intensity that draw your attention in.

Skydiving in Thailand made time slow.

So did meditating in silence.

Even walking outside with no phone allows time to stretch.

There are stories from car crash survivors who felt like time slowed. They recall being able to think strategically in those moments when things were out of control within what feels like 30 seconds is actually just 3 to 5 seconds long.

Time is also relative. As we age, each period of your life is smaller compared to your whole life. When you're 5, one year accounts for 20% of your life as opposed to when you're 50 and one year only accounts for 2% of your life. This can partially explain why time seems to speed up. This idea works in conjunction with the fact that a 5 year old will have 50 new experiences in a year vs a 50 year old who may only have 5 new experiences each year. The first theory we have no control over, but the amount of new experiences we fully control.

I see temporal awareness as honoring life's fragility. It's not just about to-do lists or time blocks. It's recognizing how precious each hour is and how the choices you make ripple outward.

You don't need more time, you need more attention inside the time you already have.

Three meditations for three dimensions of awareness. Meditation is one of the most powerful ways to practice awareness. It's ancient, rooted in traditions like Hinduism, but universally embraced for its power to calm, clarify, and center. Each type of meditation supports one dimension of awareness:

1. Breath-Focused Meditation—*Self Awareness*

Sit still. Close your eyes. Focus on the inhale and exhale. Nothing more. This practice grounds you, reduces stress, and builds internal clarity. If more direction and focus is needed. Use box breathing, 4 second inhale, 4 second hold, 4 second exhale, 4 second hold, and repeat to help your mind from wandering. Start with 30 seconds three times per week and aim to get to 5min daily.

2. Open Awareness Meditation—*Spatial Awareness*

This form invites you to observe thoughts and sensations without attachment. Let them drift through your mind like clouds across the sky. No judgement. No resistance. This builds emotional intelligence and awareness of your surroundings. Think about recent interactions, emotions, or experiences. Let the thoughts flow in and back out. What feelings, ideas, and people does your mind gravitate towards? Start with 5-10min three times per week and work your way to 10-15min daily.

3. Visualization Meditation—*Temporal Awareness*

My personal favorite. I often picture a lit candle and try to hold its image without distraction. When I first started, I could barely manage a few seconds before the image of the candle disappeared. With time, I've developed focus and mental discipline—skills that transfer directly to long-term goals. Another approach is to visualize a future reality you'd like to come to fruition.

Each of these practices reinforces one of the core principles of awareness: **Presence, Acceptance, and Focus.**

Presence helps you experience life more fully because when you're fully present you notice more.

Acceptance softens the grip of control and allows you flexibility to adjust as needed.

Focus turns attention into power, it's what turns hitting a target to getting a bullseye consistently.

Journaling: Capturing awareness in motion. If meditation sharpens awareness in the moment, journaling stores it for the future. Your mind is a powerful processor, but a terrible hard drive. Journaling clears space. It allows your thoughts to be seen, sorted, and shaped.

It helps you:

- Organize emotions

- Create space between impulse and reaction

- Identify patterns

- Enhance creativity

- Practice gratitude

Morning journaling is especially powerful because it happens before outside influence kicks in. That time, before the external news, the social notifications, or the weight of work imprints on you; morning journaling gives you access to your *purest self* first.

Some great minds: Leonardo da Vinci, Oprah, President Obama—have all sworn by the transformative power of writing. Especially on paper, which engages the mind in a way typing never can.

In 2018, a study performed by JMIR Mental Health found that participants who journaled for 15 minutes a day, 3 days per week, experienced significant improvements in their well-being and reduced anxiety after just one month. Writing about past events helps build emotional intelligence, immune systems, and a more adaptive self-narrative.

The awareness to rise. As you become more aware, you start to see how everything is connected:

- Your emotions and your decisions.

- Your thoughts and your patterns.

- Your presence and your impact.

- Your time and your transformation.

Awareness isn't a luxury. It's a responsibility. And the more you grow, the more life will demand of you. But that's not a punishment, it's a sign of your expansion.

As Frederick Douglass once said: *"If there is no struggle, there is no progress."*

Building awareness can be uncomfortable. You'll have to face truths, drop old habits, and question patterns that once felt natural. But that discomfort is the birthplace of every version of you that's yet to come.

Awareness is your compass. Not loud. Not forceful. But always guiding. You just have to be still enough to hear it.

CHAPTER 3

Persistence

Every failure is a seed; plant that seed, water that seed, grow that seed, and reap its fruit.
—RICHARD PANIER

Progress in motion. Consistency is key, and best believe it's a key that can unlock just about any door. Persistence isn't about perfection. It's about consistency: continuing forward motion, even when the terrain shifts or the finish line moves. It's not just doing, but *becoming*, through discipline, adaptability, and grit.

Persistence isn't blind repetition, it's focused resilience.

This chapter explores what it can look like to build sustainable effort, why adaptation matters just as much as consistency, and what it means to develop a mindset rooted in progress, not perfection.

The attic that built the foundation. After college, while my peers were renting high-rise NYC apartments and diving headfirst into their first taste of financial independence, I made a different choice. I moved into my great uncle's finished attic in the suburbs of Rosedale, Queens.

The ceilings were low, the space was tight, I slept on a twin bed, and my commute to work was 1.5 hours each way. On top of that, if I had late nights at the office, I'd get hit with reduced train schedules and an even longer commute. But I had a bigger goal of building passive income, so I delayed gratification of truly living on my own or commuting convenience.

I gave up weekday outings, that way I could get home to spend time analyzing real estate deals, prepare my lunch for the next day, and wake up to get a 5am workout at the nearby park then shower before catching the 6:30a bus.

I made short-term sacrifices to create long-term options. I wanted to start investing in real estate, so I learned to save 60% of my paycheck by avoiding rent costs. This allowed me to travel often without debt. I even began lending money with interest. That attic gave me a launchpad!

Today, I'm probably in the best shape of my life, I own over $3m in cash flowing assets, and became a millionaire by 30 as I planned at 22.

Now, let me pause here, because not everyone has the opportunity to live with their family rent-free. The point of this story isn't to suggest you need the *same* sacrifice, it's to inspire you to identify your *own* sacrifice.

What's your attic?

What can you temporarily give up to invest in something bigger long-term?

It could be downsizing your apartment, cutting back on brunch, getting a roommate, going back to school, a social media break to reallocate that time, waking up earlier, or picking up a side hustle. The sacrifice doesn't have to look the same, it just has to be *intentional*. Persistence starts where comfort ends. But it's only for a season, to build something meaningful for a lifetime.

Sometimes persistence means making moves that aren't glamorous, but are strategic. We often convince ourselves that letting something go or stepping outside our comfort zone won't really make a difference. But the truth is, we're not avoiding the act, we're avoiding the discomfort. And that's exactly where growth lives. Leaning into discomfort, consistently, is the training ground for transformation. Not just for a few days, but for a real stretch. Start with 30 days, but if you really want to see what you're made of, commit to 90.

Pivoting isn't quitting. Persistence doesn't mean refusing to change course. It means staying committed to the destination, even if the route changes.

For example, In 2021 I purchased a half-acre lot with a plan to subdivide it and build three modern homes. It was my first foray into development, a steep learning curve, but I was ready to learn by doing.

Then the city put a hold on my development efforts so they could rezone the neighborhood. My project was delayed 15 months. Interest payments piled up, and cash reserves started draining. Eventually, I had to pivot. I subdivided the property into 3 lots, had the plans permitted, then sold each one individually along with the building plans.

I originally purchased the property for $515,000. Put $60,000 into it. Sold each lot with the building plans for ~$300,000 each.

Did I complete the project how I set out to? No.

Did I still develop and profit from the deal? Yes.

Did I learn more than any book could teach me? Absolutely!

Persistence isn't about forcing an outcome, it's about staying open to better ones.

The 2% Rule: Compounding Progress. My mindset around persistence is grounded in a simple principle: Improve by 2% daily. That means getting better or learning something new by doing for myself, others, or profit. You can also look at it as a mental, physical, and emotional win each day. Pick three pillars that work for you.

The 2% idea stems from my background in finance. Just like compound interest can turn small deposits into large gains; small, intentional growth adds up over time. That means each day I aim to add knowledge, improve my VO2 max, or simply check on a loved one or new acquaintance. I apply this rule across the board:

- I listen to podcasts daily to keep expanding my mind. I.e. BiggerPockets, The Art of Manliness, EarnYourLeisure, Quote of the Day, DOAC, On Purpose, and The Ed Mylett show, to name a few.

- I work out or move my body every day, even if it's just a 1-hour walk on Sundays.

- In relationships, I aim for one small gesture that says, *I thought about you*, from making coffee to picking a favorite snack.

You don't have to overhaul your life in a week. You just have to keep watering the seed.

Discipline is a muscle. I once read *The Miracle Morning* by Hal Elrod, and it changed how I viewed discipline. It introduced me to the idea that discipline isn't something you *decide* on every day, it's something you *automate*. I can't make decisions based on feelings. I don't want or feel like going to the gym, but I need to go in order to have the physique I would like.

Now my mornings are wired for momentum:

- My automatic lights gradually illuminate at 4:45am.

- I sleep with a 16oz cup of water by the bed to rehydrate when I wake up.

- No phones in the bedroom or in arm's reach

- My gym clothes are laid out the night before.

By the time I fully wake up, I'm already in motion.

I also learned the power of reducing decision fatigue from greats like Steve Jobs. While I'm not wearing the same outfit every day like him, I still keep it fly, I've simplified my wardrobe and routines so I'm not burning mental energy on little things.

Discipline is a muscle and every routine is a rep that makes it stronger.

Adaptability, the hidden side of persistence. People think quitting is the opposite of persistence. It's not. Rigidity is.

Being overly committed to one method, path, or timeline will break you. Adaptability is what keeps persistence alive. It's knowing when to tweak the plan, change the pace, or shift your approach without giving up on the goal.

Like a GPS rerouting when you hit traffic or road construction:

You're still going to the destination, you're just taking the smarter path.

When it gets heavy, insert grit. To me, grit isn't about forcing your way through every obstacle. It's about *maturing* your choices to serve you even when it's hard.

It's staying the course when you want to fold.

It's showing up when no one's watching.

I don't want to but I have to.

It's making decisions that don't just feel good now, but will feel *great* later.

Grit isn't emotional flexibility, it's emotional conviction. It's your "why" you decided to accomplish something and in most cases if you don't accomplish it, your "why" wasn't powerful enough. I have everything I've really wanted and if I don't have it, then I didn't really want it.

You don't need to be cold to be focused. You just need to care deeply, and move with purpose.

The habit loop and never skipping twice. One of the most effective ways I've built persistence is through the **Habit Loop**, identified in Charles Duhigg's *The Power of Habit*:

$$\text{Cue} \longrightarrow \text{Routine} \longrightarrow \text{Reward}$$

For example, every night:

- I fill my water cup (cue)

- I drink it first thing when I wake up (routine)

- I feel energized, focused, and hydrated to go to the gym (reward)

Same goes for fitness. I follow a *never skip twice* rule. If I miss a workout one day, the next day I'm back at it, no excuses. Even when I travel, I pack enough clothes to work out at least every other day. Falling off the horse is normal. Staying off isn't because the goal is consistency not perfection.

What is a habit loop you can create in your life today for tomorrow? Do you need to sleep with your phone across the room? Should your gym clothes already be laid out or worn to bed? What cue will help you spark a routine you don't have to put much thought into?

Build what you can sustain. Persistence is a quiet power. It's not always loud. It doesn't need applause. But it's always working, growing roots, building muscle, and stretching your capacity.

- Discipline keeps you consistent.
- Adaptability keeps you flexible.
- Grit keeps you anchored.

Your future isn't shaped by one giant leap, it's shaped by thousands of small steps you refuse to stop taking.

Keep showing up.

Keep learning.

Keep planting the seeds.

Your growth is already in motion.

Persistence in Practice. Think back to a time in your life when you were persistent, when quitting would've been easier, but something in you said, *keep going.* The hardest thing you've had to overcome.

- What was the goal or situation?

- What made you stay focused (what was your *why*) despite obstacles or distractions?

- Was it internal motivation, external pressure, unseen faith, ego centered, survival need?

- What habits, people, or systems supported your persistence?

- Now bring that energy forward.

- Where in your life could you use that same level of persistence?

- What would it look like to apply that mindset to your health, your career, your relationships, or your creative projects.

Persistence is less about "I don't want to right now" and more about "That's exactly why I need to right now." Progress comes from persistent days, not perfect days.

SECTION 2

Identity

CHAPTER 4

Philosophy

"A person's life is dyed by the color of their thoughts."
—Marcus Aurelius

Philosophy is the framework for fulfillment. Your personal philosophy is the instruction manual for your life. It's the lens through which you view the world, evaluate decisions, and move toward your goals. For some, that framework is inherited through religion or culture. For others, it's shaped through lived experience, intentionally built over time.

Philosophy is dynamic. It evolves as you grow. It matures as you endure. And when clearly defined, it becomes the quiet voice that anchors you during chaotic seasons. It's the filter that simplifies decision-making. A path to overcome life's challenges.

Where it begins. One of my earliest influences was my mother. She groomed me to become someone who couldn't be easily boxed in, especially as a young Black man in America. That meant curating how I showed up in the world, even down to the smallest details. I remember asking if I could braid my hair after growing out my afro in 3rd grade, and she shut that down immediately, not out of judgment, but protection. She understood the power of perception. She knew that image and intention walk hand in hand, and she wanted mine to be clear, strong, and self-directed. It wasn't just about image, she wanted me to be well-rounded: academically, physically, and socially. Buying scholastic workbooks during the summer, putting me in tennis, basketball, and gymnastics, and allowing me to develop my own friendships while staying in touch with family.

That early lesson stuck: *Who I am begins with how I see myself, and what I stand for.*

My philosophy now is "Do well and Do Good". I didn't fully articulate my personal philosophy when it came to my career until I began working with Status: Home, Inc., a nonprofit that provides affordable housing to homeless and low-income individuals affected by HIV/AIDS. Before that, real estate was strictly a profit path, a strategy to create financial freedom. But at Status: Home, I witnessed how the very same skills that could create wealth, could also create *impact*. That was a revelation. In school I knew I didn't want to trade time for money but to allow my money to work for more money. That left me with the unknown of what to do with my own time and that's when I realized it was to make an impact on others. Showing up, supporting, being a sounding board.

Out of that season came my guiding principle:

Do well. Do good.

Do well financially because it creates options, mobility, and security for myself and family.

Do good socially by using those resources to add value to society.

Money is a universal resource. But fulfillment comes from what you *do* with it.

Helping others triggers a chemical release of oxytocin, an internal reward system that says, *this is right.*

It's not just emotionally fulfilling. It's biologically hardwired.

If you're unhappy it's because you haven't helped enough people. You don't need money to volunteer or mentor.

Gain freedom through discipline. Another core belief of mine is that true freedom is born from discipline. We often think of discipline as restriction. But in practice, discipline *unlocks* your time, energy, and potential. When you do what needs to be done, you free up mental space to enjoy what you want to do. There's no guilt of unfinished tasks lurking in the back of your mind. You can forget about the task because it's done. This allows you to truly be in the moment. Procrastination leaves a lingering guilt. That guilt costs you peace, discipline affords you peace.

Of course becoming more disciplined is easier said than done. Just like lifting heavy weights, it's not done all in the first rep but through repeated sets and progressive overload. The more you exercise discipline the easier it becomes to do more and the harder it becomes to fall off.

Discipline clears the runway so joy can land.

For me, that looks like rising early, time-blocking my day the night before, minimizing distractions, and structuring my life around what matters most. The best way I can do that is putting what needs to get done on paper and determining the top 2 priorities there. The tasks that are of high importance and biggest reward. If it's all important then figure which has the biggest reward or outcome. On a given day my first priority is going to the gym. From there I can truly tackle the day's to-do list.

Pareto's principle also known as the 80/20 principle is a great foundation. It essentially says that if you have 10 things to do and you prioritize the top two correctly, you can get an 80% return on everything you need in life. And it works in many areas, 80% of the wealth is found in the top 20% of the population. I wear 20% of my shoes 80% of the time.

Realizing this is the reason I can travel freely, invest confidently, and create without the weight of regret. Prioritization is a tool. Freedom is the reward.

Philosophical influences. Over time, my philosophy has been shaped by many thinkers and spiritual frameworks aside from Pareto. A few guiding sources:

- **Stoicism,** for its focus on self-mastery and emotional control. Responsive not reactive.

- **Ikigai,** the Japanese concept of finding purpose at the intersection of what you love, what you're good at, what the world needs, and what you can be paid for.

- **As A Man Thinketh,** for the power of thought in shaping identity. What you think is what is bound to happen.

- **Think Like a Monk,** for the peace & joy that comes from simplicity and internal clarity.

- **Omnism,** which allows me to learn from all religions without being bound by one, finding truth across traditions rather than within one doctrine.

My spirituality compass isn't tied to a single religion or structure. It's guided by what lifts me higher and grounds me deeper.

Your philosophy should act. A great philosophy isn't just an idea, it's a compass. It guides how you navigate people, problems, and purpose. It doesn't just ask "What's right for me?" but also "What's right to do?".

Here's how I apply mine:

- **Decision-making:** If I can help someone without losing something *detrimental*, I will. Win-win is the goal. Win-neutral is still meaningful. And even win-loss can be acceptable, if their win is greater than my loss.

  Win-loss may seem counterintuitive. We're taught giving more than we get is weak or unsustainable, but sometimes that's exactly what strength looks like. Think about a parent caring for a sick child in the middle of the night. There's no immediate "win" for the parent, just lost sleep, ruined schedule, and exhaustion. Yet, the child's comfort is still worth it. That's a win-loss dynamic where the magnitude of the win outweighs the loss. The same goes for volunteering.

Stay in alignment with your philosophy because there's an intrinsic reward even when there's no material return. Ask yourself is this sacrifice or self-betrayal?

- **Alignment Check:** When I'm aligned with my philosophy, I feel energized, lit up with purpose. When I'm not, I feel drained. It's not complicated, it's *felt*.

- **True Alignment:** I feel most like myself when mentoring others, volunteering time, or creating memories with loved ones. Those are the spaces where fulfillment meets flow.

Craft your philosophy. If you're reading this and wondering how to define your own guiding philosophy, here's how to begin:

1. Reflect on Core Values

What do you value most? Integrity? Curiosity? Loyalty? Growth? Write down your top five, and think about how they influence your daily decisions. Maybe even write it on your bathroom mirror.

2. Craft a Personal Mission Statement

This doesn't have to be a grand declaration, just a simple phrase that captures what drives you and how you want to impact others.

Ask:

- Why do I do what I do?

- How do I want people to feel around me?

- What impact do I want to leave?

3. Trace Your Influences

What books, moments, or people have changed how you think? Honor those lessons and keep building on them. If you can't think of any, check out the books I've recommended in this reading.

4. Practice It Daily

Philosophy isn't what you believe in theory. It's how you show up when things get hard. Try:

- **Journaling** to track alignment with your values or even planning/prioritizing your day. I do this before bed or when I first wake up so no outside information influences my thoughts.

- **Mindful reflection** to reset when you drift or process emotions. My favorite time to do this is in the sauna after each workout.

- **Seeking perspectives** that challenge and expand your view. Have some close friends whose perspective I value and trust.

My hope is that you take these lessons and shape your own path. Your passion may lie outside of real estate, and that's okay. Just remember this:

Whatever path you choose, let your philosophy be your foundation. Let it guide you in how you build, how you serve, and how you live.

Because a clear philosophy won't just help you lead. It'll help you become someone worth following.

"Your personal philosophy is the greatest determining factor in how your life works out." –Jim Rohn

CHAPTER 5

Character

*"The measure of a person's real character is what
they would do if they'd never be found out."*
–THOMAS B. MACAULAY

Who are you when no one is watching? There's a difference between being liked and being respected. One is based on charm. The other is based on consistency!

Character is who you are when no one's watching. It's the collection of daily choices, moral reflexes, and value-driven actions that form your true identity. While philosophy is your instruction manual, character is the internal framework that determines how you respond: to pressure, to people, and to power.

It doesn't form in a moment. It's shaped over time. And it's proven, not proclaimed. Reputation is built in the spotlight. Character is built in the dark.

The quiet choices that matter. There are certain things I just do, no fanfare and no expectation of praise.

I open doors for every woman who gets in the car with me, whether it's a family member, a date, or a friend. And I do the same for everyone when we walk into a building together. That's part Southern upbringing, part being raised around women, and part belief that respect should be felt, not just spoken.

I also clean up, if I eat at someone's home, I'll help do the dishes. If I see trash on the ground and there's a bin nearby, I'll throw it away. Not because I have to, but because I believe in leaving anyone and anything better than I found them.

Character is revealed in the things you do when there's no reward attached.

One of my best friends, Solomon, often tweets each morning: *"Everything I touch will be successful."* It's more than a mantra, it's a mindset. And I've adopted a version of it myself. I believe everything and everyone I come across should be better in some way because of our interaction. Whether it's leaving a space cleaner, a friend more confident, a smile shared, or a stranger feeling seen, I carry a quiet conviction:

If I touch it, I help it grow. If I meet you, I hope I've added value, even if that's just in the form of a laugh.

The quiet choices show up in the way you return a shopping cart. The way you stack your plates after a meal at a restaurant. The way you have difficult conversations with friends when it would be easier to stay silent. These aren't headline moments, but they shape how the world experiences you.

What I look for in others... When I think about character in others, three traits stand out: **Consideration. Honesty. Genuineness.**

Consideration because I trust people who can be attuned to the needs of others, even when they don't directly benefit. Honesty because I respect people who tell the truth even when it's uncomfortable, but without weaponizing it. Lastly, I admire those who are genuine enough to offer honesty and care, not just when there's something to gain.

Too often, people reserve their best behavior for moments where they can be seen. But real character isn't selective. It's consistent. More often their best behavior is saved for strangers and loved ones get the short end of the stick. You treat your boss nicer than your partner or more pleasant with a stranger than your parents or kids.

Discipline, humility, and integrity. These three values guide my daily character. Discipline is the foundation. It's showing up even when you don't feel like it. Whether it's my fitness routine, my personal development habits, or how I manage my time, discipline keeps me rooted. You can't claim you've been doing the work if your results don't reflect it. Just like numbers don't lie, disciplined living shows up in your habits and outcomes.

Humility is the posture. I believe it's either stay humble or be humbled. Reading *How to Win Friends & Influence People* taught me the power of making space for others: asking questions, complimenting genuinely, and giving the freedom to share who they are. It also made me hyperaware of those I need to limit my time with. People who only talk about themselves, offer criticism that isn't constructive, or seek praise/credit especially without giving it. Humility is subtle confidence. It's knowing your value without needing to prove it in every room you enter.

Integrity is the legacy. Your name travels further than your feet ever will. When people speak about you in rooms you haven't entered, let it be with respect. Whether they've observed your interactions, heard your story, or worked with you directly, your integrity is your stamp. And you only get one.

Reflect often. I replay conversations, scan decisions, and think about reactions I could improve next time. Most of the time, when I feel disappointed in myself, it's tied to *impatience*. Moments where I spoke too quickly, assumed too much, or reacted before reflecting.

The moments I'm proudest of? When I have grace, to others or to myself. When I was patient enough to allow clarity to catch up to emotion. When I respond with care rather than control.

Character isn't about never messing up. It's about how you respond when you do.

We are built by environment and refined by choice. I grew up in a single-mother household, surrounded mostly by women: cousins, aunts, and eventually, two younger sisters. I had strong examples of care, resilience, and strength from an early age. I also saw how much unseen labor women carry and how simple acts of consideration can go a long way.

My parents were both generous and supportive, always modeling the importance of giving to others. But character, for me, wasn't shaped by one person. It was built through observations, tested in experiences, and refined through reflections. As Haitian immigrants, my parents took in family and friends who made their way to the States. I watched them provide food, shelter, transportation, and resources to land jobs until they could get on their own to support themselves.

Remember, character is a daily practice. You don't "have" good character. You practice it. Not once in a while. Not just when it's convenient. But daily, in the little things, in the quiet moments, and in the choices no one else notices.

There's a mantra among Navy SEALs:

Earn your trident every day. And as soon as you get out you're no longer a SEAL but a former Navy SEAL.

It's the same with character. You don't get to wear the badge if you're not living the code. Character is how you build trust without saying a word. It's how you lead without shouting. It's how you love without needing credit.

So ask yourself often:

- Am I doing what I said I would?

- Am I being who I said I am?

- Am I moving like someone whose name deserves respect?

What do you do when no one is watching? Who are you when your back is against the wall? How do you show up for others?

Because in the end, the loudest thing about you will be the quiet example you leave behind.

CHAPTER 6

Personality

"Personality begins where comparison leaves off.
Be unique. Be memorable. Be confident."
–Shannon L. Alder

The expression of you. Personality is the way your soul introduces itself to the world. It's not only how you act, it's how your values show up in motion. It's how you make people feel, how you communicate, and how you color the spaces you enter. If character is your internal framework, then personality is the voice, the tempo, and the rhythm you travel by.

It's both inherited and shaped. Part instinct, part experience. Some pieces of it remain steady across your life, others evolve as you grow, adapt, and connect more intentionally.

Warm like a hug, yet lively like a dance. If I had to describe my personality, I'd say it's exactly that. I'm not usually the loudest in the room, but my presence is felt. People often tell me I make them feel safe and that's something I hold with gratitude. I tend to observe the energy of a space before I speak, reading moods, and taking in dynamics before stepping in. At FAMU, I was the host of an on-campus TV show called Behind the Suit. I interviewed students who had an interesting story to tell but you'd never know cause we were all dressed alike in business attire. This experience taught me how to be an active listener and the art of the follow up question.

When I lead, I do so with charisma, intention, and clarity around other people's goals. Whether it's in work, community, or friendship I love connecting people to others on a similar path or to ideas that stretch their thinking. One of my greatest joys is nudging people slightly outside their comfort zone and watching them light up once they realize they're in a space they were meant for all along.

I recharge by sticking to my personal rhythm: working out, getting sunlight, journaling, and being around people who allow me to be myself, without having to be all polished or performative.

Rooted in reflection, refined through learning. One thing that's always been consistent is my interest in others. I've always loved hearing people's stories: what makes them tick, what excites them, and what shaped their path.

As a kid, I moved around a lot with my mother. That constant change in environment meant I was regularly the "new kid". I had to learn how to read a room quickly, adapt, and make new friends. Over time, this sharpened my ability to connect with different types of people. It also made me deeply curious about what made others feel seen, included, and understood.

I had plenty of cousins and friends I ran around with, but at home it was just my mom and me. I was an only child until I was ten, but even then I didn't live with my siblings until I was fifteen. Fifteen years of solitude taught me how to enjoy my own company. I'd entertain myself and reflect, building a relationship with my inner world long before I had the language for it.

Even now, I'm often perceived as an extrovert because of how I carry myself socially. But truth be told, I value alone time just as much. On weekends I may host friends, go to events, or bring people together. But during the week, I'm in my space quietly working, reflecting, or restoring.

My understanding of personality deepened as I matured. I started to intentionally study how people think, behave, and connect. *How to Win Friends & Influence People*, *Attached*, *Predictably Irrational*, *The Way of the Superior Man*, *Maybe You Should Talk to Someone*, *Personality isn't Permanent*, and *Talking to Strangers* helped me deepen both self-awareness and my ability to understand others.

Your personality isn't just how you are seen, but also how others see themselves when they're around you.

There are frameworks for connection. To better understand how personality plays a role in relationships, I've leaned on a few frameworks by some renowned researchers:

- **Attachment Styles**: How we form bonds and react to emotional closeness, often shaped in childhood. This helped me maneuver how I show up in relationships. Learning the difference between an avoidant, anxious, and secure attachment style. Being intentional about becoming secure through therapy and journaling. Quiz can be found online.

- **Love Languages**: How we express and receive love through words, time, acts, gifts, or touch. Dr. Gary Chapman developed this while working as a marriage counselor and noticing recurring themes during sessions. Acts of service is my top way to receive and show love but we must consider how the other person prefers to receive love.

- **Apology Languages**: How we like to be reconciled. The options are via change, responsibility, restitution, regret, or expression. With the help of Jennifer Thomas, this was based on a similar methodology to love languages and has some great benefits when navigating conflict.

These tools don't define who we are, but they give language to how we relate. When two people are aware of their differences or similarities, they can better show up with patience, clarity, and compassion.

Gentleness is a power. If there's one trait people often don't expect from me, it's gentleness. Maybe it's because I can come across as stoic when I first enter a space. Maybe it's because our culture doesn't always associate masculinity with softness. But the truth is, I'm deeply nurturing. I listen intently. I give freely. I'm attentive by nature. That gentleness is not a weakness, it's a strength that grounds my personality in humility and care.

Gentleness isn't the absence of power. It's power with control. It's presence with empathy.

Personality shows leadership and love. Personality plays a massive role in leadership. It influences how people respond to your direction, whether they feel empowered or invisible. It's not just about being likable, it's about being *trustworthy*. In my experience, the best leaders understand how their personality sets the emotional tone for everyone around them.

In relationships, personality matters just as much. It affects how you resolve conflict, how you celebrate wins, how you interpret silence. Dr. John Gottman outlines in his Four Horsemen model the destructive communication patterns: criticism, defensiveness, contempt, and stonewalling can derail even the strongest of partnerships. Awareness of your personality gives you the insight to avoid those traps and the empathy to meet your partner or even a friend halfway.

Sometimes our personalities bring out the best in each other. Other times, they clash and someone ends up dimming their light to make the relationship "work." That's why it's so important to know yourself. To know how you naturally respond to stress, joy, disappointment, and success. To know when you need space and when to speak up.

When you understand your own energy, you become more intentional in every space you enter and every connection you make.

Your vibe is your invitation. Your personality is not your whole identity, but it's the part others get to experience most. It's how your inner world reaches the outer world. How you say "this is who I am" without using those words.

Whether gentle or bold, introspective or expressive, your personality is a vehicle for impact. But it only works if you know how to drive it. If you understand your traits, tendencies, and triggers. If you stay aligned with what energizes you, and aware of what drains you.

Your personality is your vibe.

Your vibe is your invitation.

And the right people, opportunities, and experiences will always RSVP when you show up as your full self.

SECTION 3

Exploration

CHAPTER 7

Curiosity

"Stay hungry. Stay foolish."
—STEVE JOBS

The spark of exploration. I didn't realize it then, but my mother was quietly handing me Blue's Clues to discover myself, one new experience at a time. Guitar, Boy Scouts, baseball, skating, tennis, and board games. She kept my schedule full not just for structure, but for something more foundational: **curiosity**. She knew that exposure was the on-ramp to identity. That trying new things wasn't about mastery—it was about possibility. She wasn't trying to mold me into a prodigy, she was tilling the soil so that I could grow into one. And that's what curiosity does, it offers us a thousand ways to knock on the door of who we might be.

Curiosity builds identity. From a young age, I was learning to explore. I traveled to Haiti, visited family along the East Coast, explored the neighborhood with friends on bikes as a kid, and through the Center for Global Security & International

Affairs at FAMU. I found myself walking through places I never imagined: Brazil, South Africa, Lesotho, and Swaziland. I stood at the headquarters of the CIA and FBI in Virginia, not because I had the most impressive resume, but because I told myself to say *yes* to every opportunity that aligned with who I, at the time, wanted to become.

That *yes* came from curiosity. I've often said: "Connections get you in the room. Curiosity keeps you there."

Imagine, you're at your grandparents' house. You look out the window and see your grandmother in the backyard. You're young, so you wander outside and ask, "What are you doing?" She smiles, waves you over, and starts showing you how she tills the soil, cares for her tomatoes, keeps the bugs away. That simple moment, sparked by curiosity, gets you invited into the garden. You didn't have a skillset or a reason to be there. You just had a question. Curiosity keeps you in the room. And if you're open, life will show you what it's growing.

Curiosity says yes to aligned experiences. In college, I kept this mindset of openness. I said yes to the Center for Global Security trip. That yes led me to the southern hemisphere, to embassies and dirt roads, to conversations in Portuguese and Zulu. None of those experiences were required for my major. They were simply aligned with where I believed my future could lead: global impact. Curiosity, when rooted in alignment, becomes a compass. It doesn't just chase what's shiny. It notices what resonates. And that resonance is powerful. It's what pulled me into leadership positions and took me from Executive Assistant of NABA to two-time President, from attending an informational to student ambassador for PwC, from chivalry to male representative for the National Council of Negro Women at FAMU. It wasn't just credentials that got me there. It was curiosity paired with charisma. The willingness to ask, *What's going on here?* And the ability to lean in with humility and enthusiasm.

From curious to capable: Learning by doing. Curiosity also pushes you to build. I despised the costs of textbooks, so I once had the business idea to convert every textbook into an e-book. Mind you this is back in 2010. I ran into publishing roadblocks, and rather than give up entirely, I pivoted, creating an on-campus textbook exchange so students wouldn't have to keep buying overpriced books. I was just trying to scratch an itch. It wasn't the million-dollar idea, but it was the right idea for that moment. That's what curiosity does. It doesn't always give you success, but it gives you momentum. And momentum is what builds capability. You don't figure it all out before you start; you figure it out by starting.

Career, Calling, and Contribution. I've come to see there are three layers to how we show up in the world:

- A **career** is what you do to make a living. It's your skills that translate into income.

- A **calling** is what you do because it calls something out of you, your purpose, your gifts, your heart for others.

- A **contribution** is the broader impact you make through how you make others feel, what you leave behind, and who you lift as you climb.

My career is in real estate. My calling became affordable housing. And my contribution is the legacy I'm building for my family and my community through ownership, access, and education.

Curiosity leads to purpose. Some experiences make you feel alive. Others make you feel *on purpose*. When I went skydiving in Thailand, I felt electric, like nothing could stop me. But when I helped close deals for Status: Home, preserving affordable housing for real people in real need, that felt like purpose. When I took my younger sisters on siblings trips to Peru, Colombia, Germany, France, Spain, and Singapore that felt like contribution. That felt like growth coming full circle. Those moments happened because of curiosity. Because I chose to till the soil. And that's what curiosity does, it offers us a thousand ways to knock on the door of who we might be.

Stay hungry. Stay Curious. You were born curious. That hasn't changed. Curiosity is how you learned to crawl, to walk, to speak. It's how you discovered your favorite color, your favorite music, your favorite kind of people. Somewhere along the way, society told us we had to narrow down, specialize, lock in. But in reality, new experiences are the entire purpose of young adulthood, of any age really.

Try it.

Explore it.

Be around people who love it and see if you love it too.

If it aligns with your values or your vision, say yes, even if you don't know all the details yet.

Curiosity isn't about answers, it's about possibility. Anything you haven't done yet isn't because you can't. It's just because you haven't figured out how.

Stay open.

Stay curious.

The garden is waiting.

CHAPTER 8

Alignment

*"Don't [just] ask what the world needs. Ask what
makes you come alive and go do that. Because what
the world needs is people who come alive."*
—Howard Thurman

Where curiosity meets contribution. Connections get you in the room. Alignment helps you decide whether you should stay. Back in my day, I said yes to just about everything. Guitar lessons, Boy Scouts (lasted a day, hated it), baseball, campus leadership, global travel, startup ventures, I was tilling the soil, testing environments, and planting seeds without knowing which ones would grow. I'm grateful for that season. It gave me range, but eventually, something shifts.

You start to ask better questions:

Does this energize me?

Will it matter in five years?

Is this aligned with the person I'm becoming or the one I'm outgrowing?

That's when exploration becomes intentional. That's when curiosity grows roots and becomes alignment.

When you're the first to go first. Alignment often begins in moments when you don't yet feel ready, but you show up anyway. My parents didn't attend a four year college. Thanks to my bonus mom I was on my way to FAMU with a suitcase full of scholarships. Accompanied with my ambition and good intentions, but still I had no real roadmap. My first year, my grades reflected that. I was adjusting to a new environment, trying to figure out who I was, what I wanted, and where I fit.

Eventually, I found my rhythm, by reaching out. I connected with upperclassmen, professors, and recruiters. I learned how to move in the room. Then I learned how to *lead* in the room. I spoke up in class and volunteered to present. I saw college experience as practice. To be prepared for the real world, when there were real dollars at stake. If you don't speak up in the classroom, you won't speak up in the boardroom.

Becoming president of NABA taught me that alignment isn't always found, it's built. I didn't just run meetings, I raised over $25,000 from corporate sponsors (the dean wasn't too happy about that). I launched student development programs, helped others land internships, and even hosted my own talk show in the business school. I learned what it meant to pour into others. And in doing so, I was actually pouring into myself.

Sometimes you don't find your purpose. You help someone else reach theirs and discover yours along the way.

Learning by doing. Growing by giving. My most significant growth hasn't just come from chasing personal success. It comes from **doing the work and sharing what I know**, especially when I didn't have all the answers.

I started speaking with my circle of friends of my plans to start investing in real estate once we graduated college. I stayed after campus events to help students tweak their resumes. After a couple of deals, I later started a Patreon to teach others about personal finance and real estate. I uploaded videos to walk people through what I had to figure out on my own. Not because I needed applause but because I remembered how it felt to be at the starting line, wondering what I didn't know to ask.

Helping others win gives you more than credibility, it gives you clarity.

The more you give, the more you understand what's worth giving to and what's worth giving up.

The alignment filter. Here's how I evaluate whether something's worth my time or energy now:

1. Does it energize me?
   Not just excite, but truly *energize* me? Do I feel more alive after doing it?

2. Are there long-term benefits?
    For me and for others? Is this building something lasting
    or just feeding the moment?

If it checks both boxes, that's alignment.

If it checks neither, it's noise.

And if it checks one but not the other? It's probably a *phase*, and
that's okay too.

*Alignment isn't about perfection, it's about resonance. When
something hits just right, you know it's worth your time.*

From Costa Rica to Commitment. I'll never forget my first
solo trip to Costa Rica at 24yo. It was freeing, thrilling, and a
little unplanned. I did the research, booked the flights, mapped
out a few key sights but everything else? I winged it.

I made friends from around the world, people I still keep in
touch with today. A couple I met at my hostel even hosted me
in Amsterdam the following year. I decided to backpack solo
for several months. That trip showed me the kind of person I
wanted to be: resourceful, open, brave, and relational. Traveling
alone really allowed me to see who I was without the input of
others. My commitment was to learning who I was without the
influence of friends. As we age we don't realize how much of
our day to day is affected by our circle. My worldview becomes
a blank canvas for my thoughts and experiences to paint.

Solo travel taught me that alignment isn't found in routine. It's found in risk, in new environments, with new people, solving new problems.

The unfamiliar has a way of revealing what's essential.

Jumping without a net (and landing on purpose).

At 25, I bought my first multifamily property, a 10-unit split between two buildings. I didn't even see it in person before closing, I was in Barcelona hostel at the time when I got the call from my realtor in Tallahassee.

But I had done the work, I was prepared for this opportunity. I lined up inspections, analyzed the cash flow statements, had a little over $30,000 saved and secured $45,000 from a mentor turned friend to help fund the $75,000 down payment. I searched reviews and found a property manager online and made it happen.

That experience wasn't about proving anything. It was about alignment.

All the books I had read, podcasts I had listened to, and single-family deals I had done were leading me toward that moment. Even with that I still didn't have all of the answers but I had the gumption to get the answers as I was going.

I wasn't *buying a building*, I was stepping into the next version of myself.

And that's what alignment does.

It transforms knowledge into action.

Curiosity into conviction.

Potential into proof.

Move with meaning. There's a difference between motion and movement. You can be busy and go nowhere. Or you can move with meaning, toward something that aligns with who you are and what you were built to do. Productivity > Busy.

Curiosity tills the soil. But alignment is when you decide what to plant, where to plant, and what's worth growing.

Don't just follow your interests, follow your impact. When you align your energy with purpose, the world opens up in ways hustle alone never could.

You can do anything, but you can't do everything. Choose the things that whisper to your soul.

CHAPTER 9

Purposeful Experimentation

"You don't have to be great to start, but
you have to start to be great."
–Zig Ziglar

Growth in motion. In the early stages of adulthood, we're energized. We've gathered knowledge, explored our identity, made some decisions, and now we're ready to build something. The only problem is, we often don't know exactly what that "something" is yet.

That's okay.

The truth is, *none* of us have it all figured out when we begin.

But the people who grow, evolve, and succeed? They don't wait for clarity, they experiment with purpose.

Learning by doing, not just deciding. I once thought my path was set: I'd work on Wall Street, earn big, and transition those funds into real estate investments. It sounded solid. I met with JPMorgan, secured the job, and began building my future.

But the longer I was there, the more I realized I was giving up my *present* to fund my future. The job was structured, stable, respected, but it wasn't aligned. I felt confined, more so suffocation than sacrifice. After two and half years, it started to get to me: the commute, being stuck in a cubicle, and the cold winters.

So I pivoted and left the firm to transition to Atlanta but only after a few months of backpacking.

I didn't abandon the goal, I just changed the route. I stayed curious. I evaluated how I could still reach financial freedom and impact others, but on terms that aligned with my energy, my gifts, and my peace of mind. That shift required courage, but more importantly, it required experimentation.

I had to learn through doing, without becoming attached to any one title, job, or path.

Redefining failure. We're taught early on to avoid failure, to aim for the A, to fear the F. But in reality, failure is not the enemy of success, it's the soil it grows from. It can explain why most successful entrepreneurs and CEOs weren't all A students but the ones who learned from their failures. I've learned that fear is just "False Evidence Appearing Real." I made a C in Intermediate Accounting but it wasn't the end of the world.

Thomas Edison didn't credit himself for inventing the light bulb. He credited himself with discovering a thousand ways the light bulb *didn't* work. That mindset stuck with me.

I've come to believe that failure isn't something to be feared.

It's something to be done efficiently.

Fail fast.

Fail forward.

Fail with purpose.

Success is the star at the top of the tree, but failure is every branch that supports it. The goal isn't just to avoid missteps, it's to learn from them, adjust, and keep going. That's how you earn compound interest on your effort.

Running from failure only delays success.

When the path gets bumpy. One of the most challenging and educational experiments I've tried was getting into real estate development. I had been buying and managing existing properties, but I wanted to build from the ground up cause the market for rehabs was trash. So I bought three lots, two in Atlanta, one in Tallahassee. In hindsight, I probably should've started with one to get my feet wet.

It was a new world: zoning laws, permit delays, neighborhood planning units.

- One lot had a flawed survey.

- Another required the city to rezone the neighborhood before I could subdivide the land, delaying the project for 15 months.

- Meanwhile, interest and holding costs started eating into my cash reserves.

Did I feel overwhelmed? Absolutely.

Did I learn more than I ever could from a podcast or course? Without a doubt.

Would I do it again? Yes, but with better pacing and preparation. Looking back I bought too many lots at once, I should have either partnered with someone experienced or taken on less at the start.

That's the point of purposeful experimentation. You try with intention. You adjust without ego. You focus on the goal.

Aimless Exploration vs. Purposeful Experimentation. There's a clear difference. **Aimless exploration** feels like walking in circles. You're moving, but you're unsure where you're going. You fear committing, so you dabble, drift with loose timelines, and avoid the discomfort of growth.

Purposeful experimentation, on the other hand, says: *I don't have all the answers, but I'm going to try this and see what I learn.* Your 20s and earlier is the age to really do so because you have so much time to adjust and recover.

- It's not about chasing trends, it's about testing your truth.

- It's not about needing perfection, it's about seeking feedback.

- It's not about proving anything, it's about discovering something.

Ego says, "I should already know this."

Curiosity says, "Let's see what I can learn here."

You don't have to know, you just have to try. By now, you've learned a lot about yourself. You've sharpened your mindset, explored your identity, and found what aligns with your energy and purpose. But that doesn't mean you've arrived.

This part of life isn't about mastery, it's about motion.

Start the business.

Pitch the idea.

Buy the property.

Take the solo trip.

Record the podcast episode that only three people listen to.

Write the first page of the book.

You don't need a perfect plan to take the first step. You just need the will to try.

Stay in motion. These years, your 20s, your 30s, even your 40s, are fertile ground for experimentation. The stakes are never lower than they are right now. The risk of trying is far less than the regret of wondering *what if.*

The most valuable skill you can have in this season isn't perfection. It's **adaptability**.

You won't get it all right. You're not supposed to. But the compound interest on your effort only starts if you stay in motion.

Stay curious. Stay intentional.

Stay humble enough to try and wise enough to pivot.

You've tilled the soil.

You've planted with purpose.

Now keep experimenting.

The harvest will come.

"The master has failed more times than the beginner has even tried." –Stephen McCrani

ABOUT THE AUTHOR

RICHARD-ANTHONY PANIER is a real estate developer, fitness enthusiast, free thinker, and self-proclaimed chef dedicated to helping individuals build internal discipline before external success. Raised in a Haitian household and shaped by frequent relocation throughout childhood, Richard learned early how to adapt, observe, and grow in unfamiliar environments.

After earning his degree from Florida A&M University's School of Business and beginning his career in finance, he transitioned into real estate development, where imagination met execution. His work and writing explore the philosophy of growth: how habits, emotional intelligence, financial literacy, and spiritual grounding compound over time.

Through his book series beginning with Emerge Into Growth, Richard reframes personal development as architecture, built through intentional stress, reflection, and intentional action.

He speaks on modern masculinity, resilience, wealth-building, and the psychology of long-term success.